FEEDS AND FEEDING

by

Mary Gordon Watson

Illustrations by

Carole Vincer

THRESHOLD BOOKS

First published in Great Britain by
Threshold Books, The Kenilworth Press Limited
Addington, Buckingham, MK18 2JR

Reprinted 1989, 1991

© Threshold Books Ltd 1988

Typeset by Rapid Communications Ltd,
London WC1

Printed in England by Westway Offset

British Library Cataloguing in Publication Data

Gordon-Watson, Mary
    Feeds and Feeding.
    1. Livestock. Horses. Feeding.
    I Title   II Vincer, Carole.
    636.1′084

    ISBN 0-901366-37-4

CONTENTS

Introduction

All horses need food to develop, to replace body wastes, and to stay in good condition. It also gives them energy for work. Grass is their natural food, but it has to be replaced and supplemented for horses that are stabled, or wintering out.

There is a wider variety of horse feeds available than ever before, with scientifically prepared mixtures and compounds, and specially treated grain. These can provide a healthy diet, and make feeding easier for horse owners, but the simplest solution is not always the best one for a particular horse. Most of them are fussy feeders. The questions of what to feed, how much, and when, are best answered by the horse himself, by his appetite and his well-being.

The skill of good feeding lies in understanding the individual needs of each horse or pony, taking into account his type, age, size, temperament, physical condition, and the work required of him. It will also depend on whether he is stabled all the time, some of the time, or kept out in a field, as well as the time of year, the amount of grass available, and whether he is clipped and rugged.

Just as it is difficult for experts to agree about the best human diets, there will always be arguments about how to feed a horse. In this book, we set out the choices, make recommendations, and point out the dangers, based on the important principles of good feeding, which are the same as they have always been.

The Rules of Feeding

Horse feed consists of ROUGHAGE, such as grass and hay, for bulk and essential fibre to aid the digestion process; and CONCENTRATES, which provide energy.

The correct mixture of roughage and concentrates must be balanced carefully, according to the individual horse, his weight, age, and type of exercise.

The following rules apply to *all* feeding:

- *Feed 'little and often'.* Horses in their natural state graze almost continuously. This suits their limited stomach capacity and gradual digestive system. Large feeds of concentrates must contain fibre to slow down the eating process. Eating too much, too quickly, overloads the stomach, causing severe indigestion or colic.
- *Always water before feeding,* but it is better to have fresh, clean water available at all times—the horse is then unlikely to drink too much at once, from thirst. More than half of a horse's body weight is water. He needs it to digest and absorb food, and can drink more than 8 gallons (40 litres) in a day.
- *Feed only good-quality hay and grain.* This will prove an economy: the horse will benefit more and need less.
- *Do not make sudden changes of diet,* and *keep to regular feed times.* A horse's digestive system adapts and works best to a routine, and the balance can easily be upset, causing colic, filled legs, azoturia or other problems.
- *Never work a horse fast soon after a full feed,* or too much grass. A bulging stomach presses on the lungs, causing laboured breathing and distress.
- *Keep buckets and mangers clean*—remove leftovers.
- *Store feed in a clean, dry container* to avoid vermin, mould or possible contamination.
- *Protect feed and hay from rain or damp ground.* Make sure the feed shed is waterproof.
- *Worm your horse regularly,* and *have his teeth checked,* otherwise good food may be wasted and worthless.

Roughage, or 'Soft' Food

Grass, or *grass products*, provide the bulky foundation food that horses need. Its quality will depend on how it is managed, and the types of grasses grown. The best grass also makes the best *hay*, which is cut, dried grass, preserved for long-term use. It is the most used food for stabled horses, or those wintering out, and it keeps the same nutritional value throughout the year. Most ponies and non-working horses could be maintained entirely on top-class hay.

Silage is wet cut grass, preserved in its juices. It is not always palatable.

Horse-hage (or haylage, or hayage), a cross between hay and silage, is made specifically for horses and preserved with 50% moisture. It is highly nutritious and helps to prevent allergies to dust and fungal spores in hay. It can replace hay entirely as the horse's bulk feed, but introduce it gradually, especially a high-protein variety. Horse-hage can be mixed with hay to increase volume and make it last longer.

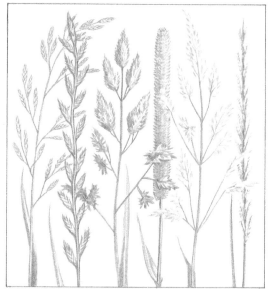

Good grasses include (*from left to right*): meadow fescue, rye-grass, cocksfoot, timothy, Yorkshire fog and purple moor grass.

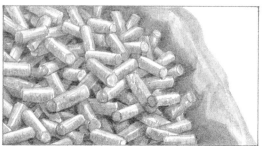

(*Above*) **Grass pellets**, a compound of dried grass, make a valuable winter supplement.
(*Below*) **Horse-hage** is specially grown grasses, vacuum-packed in polythene sacks.

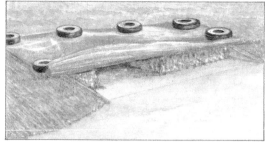

Silage is only suitable for horses when free of decay and mould. Ideally, it should be fed mixed in with two-thirds hay, but it is messy and difficult to handle. (*Below*) Silage pit.

Hay

Hay is best when the grass has been cut after flowering but before producing seeds. It should contain good, nutritious grasses and not weeds and thistles. Hay taken off neglected pasture will lack goodness.

Good-quality meadow hay is better value than inferior seed hay. Never feed mouldy or musty hay—it could seriously damage a horse's respiratory system.

A good bale should fall apart when the string is cut. Beware of dust, or damp, dark patches. Hay less than six months old could be indigestible, and might cause colic.

Chopped-up hay, or **chaff**, is ideal roughage to mix with grain. It makes a horse masticate well and aids digestion. Oat straw can provide a non-rich fibrous chaff.

Meadow hay is taken from permanent pasture and should contain many nourishing herbs and flowers. It is softer, lighter, and greener than seed hay, and usually less nutritious.

Seed hay is a specially cultivated crop of nutritious grasses such as timothy, rye, clover, and sanfoin. It is hard and crisp to touch, and sweet to smell.

Mouldy or **mow-burnt** hay is not palatable or safe to feed. It may have overheated in the rick if baled before its juicy stems had dried, or it may have been rained on.

Concentrates, or 'Hard' Food

Concentrates like oats and barley are highly nutritious, but low in fibre. They should not be fed alone; to obtain the full benefit from grain, it should be mixed with some bulk food so that it is digested slowly.

Oats give energy, and they are the ideal grain for horses, being digestible and light, but they should be bruised or rolled to prevent hungry or greedy horses from bolting them too fast, and to allow very young horses to chew them easily.

Flaked micronised *Barley* provides energy and bulk. It often replaces oats as the basic grain ration.

Wheat grain is *not* suitable, unless crushed or boiled, and fed in small quantities. It absorbs water, swells, and causes colic.

Bran, a by-product of wheat, is added to concentrates, for bulk, but has little real food value. Fed dry, it is binding and not easy to digest; fed wet, it is mildly laxative. A fit, hard-fed horse will benefit from a bran mash if he is lame or confined to his stable.

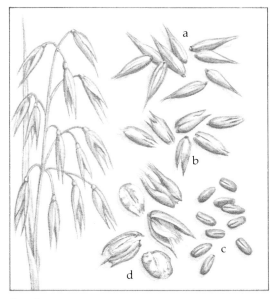

Good-quality **oats** are clean, plump and hard. They are fed (a) whole, (b) rolled, (c) clipped, or (d) bruised—but they lose nutritional value if too heavily crushed.

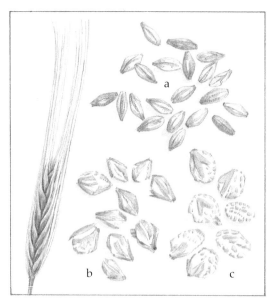

Barley – (a) whole, (b) crushed, (c) flaked. It is more fattening than oats. Never feed whole barley unless it is boiled first, as the grain is too hard.

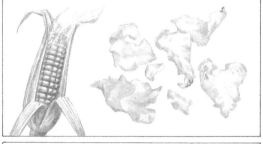

(*Above*) Flaked **maize** is fattening and provides warmth and energy, but too much could overheat the blood. (*Below*) **Bran** is fed as a bulky supplement or as a mash.

Nuts, Mixes and Supplements

Nuts, cubes, and coarse mixes (compound feeds) comprise a variety of ingredients scientifically prepared to suit every type of horse and pony. Compounds are standardised and provide a well-balanced diet containing recommended foods and vitamins. They are economical to store and transport, and need no mixing.

Nuts are less 'hotting up' than oats. However, individually prepared feeds can be more appetising, more adaptable, and less expensive.

Complete nuts combine concentrates and roughage as a total diet. This makes feeding easy, and helps to prevent allergies to hay and dust, but more natural roughage would aid their digestion.

Concentrate nuts, contain varying amounts of protein, energy, vitamins and minerals. They may be fed on their own with hay, or mixed with grain.

Coarse mixes contain cereals such as oats, barley, and maize, with linseed, beans, molasses, grassmeal, minerals and vitamins.

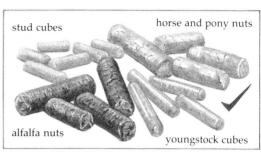

stud cubes   horse and pony nuts
alfalfa nuts   youngstock cubes

SUGAR-BEET MUST BE SOAKED FOR 12 HOURS

(*Above*) **Assorted nuts and cubes.**
(*Below*) **Sugar-beet nuts and pulp**, an appetising supplement. If not thoroughly soaked can swell in the stomach and cause colic.

(*Above*) A **coarse mix** (*left*). **Molassine meal**, or liquid molasses (*right*), is an energy-giving appetiser. (*Below*) **Linseed**, fed in tea or jelly form, is *poisonous unless cooked*.

Salt, minerals and **vitamins** are only fed when known to be lacking. **Milk pellets**, or powder, are mainly for breeding stock. **Succulents** like sliced carrots and apples add variety.

Feeding a Horse at Grass

Most horses and ponies are content in a well-maintained field from May to September, eating only grass, their natural food. Some may get too fat unless it is limited.

Between October and April, however, grass has scarcely any nutritive value, so extra feeding is essential.

A horse needs enough bulk throughout the year to keep him warm and healthy. Good-quality hay will not be wasted. All but the hardiest ponies will need concentrates, too, during the winter, especially a working horse as he uses up valuable energy in keeping warm.

Horses kept on over-grazed, weedy land will lose condition and should be fed, whatever the season.

Use a separate bowl for each horse, and space them well apart to avoid fighting and bullying. Always feed at the same times—afternoon is best, before a long, cold night.

Remember, horses *must* have a constant supply of fresh water. They also need regular worming.

Bad pasture causes hunger, worms, loss of condition, and mineral deficiencies. If a horse appears listless, gnaws wood or eats earth, he needs a change of diet—or field.

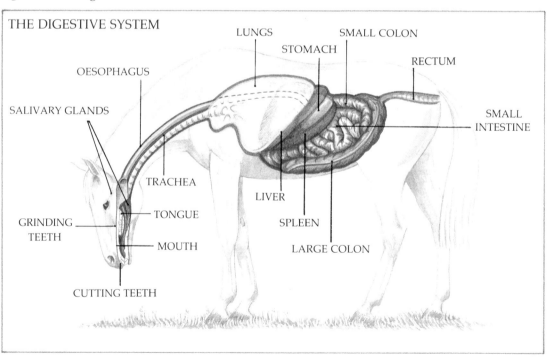

THE DIGESTIVE SYSTEM

LUNGS
STOMACH
SMALL COLON
RECTUM
OESOPHAGUS
SALIVARY GLANDS
SMALL INTESTINE
TRACHEA
LIVER
GRINDING TEETH
TONGUE
SPLEEN
MOUTH
LARGE COLON
CUTTING TEETH

Feeding the Stabled Horse

The stabled horse will adapt to an artificial diet if the basic rules of feeding are followed. He should always have some food passing through his system, but not a lot at once. Roughage is essential to assist digestion. The amount of hay, or horse-hage, will depend on the individual and the work he is doing.

'Hard', concentrated food is necessary for horses that are working, growing, or need conditioning and warmth. Appetising succulents and green food provide some natural nutrition.

Small ponies can survive on hay alone when not working hard.

No horse should be made to work on a full stomach, so leave one to two hours for digestion after feeding.

Do not feed immediately if he returns from exercise hot and sweating, or exhausted after a hard day—he will not be able to digest it.

If a horse has to be confined to his stable without exercise, concentrates must be reduced, or cut out altogether, and replaced with more bulk, otherwise he may 'seize up'.

A permanent manger is more practical than a portable container, which may tip over and has to be removed after feeding. All mangers must be kept very clean.

Before giving the horse his feed, it should be measured out carefully and mixed well. Use a scoop or measure to judge quantities. Scales are also helpful.

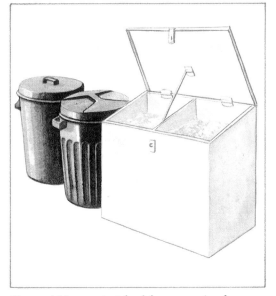

Covered bins protect feed from vermin, damp and dust. Keep different foods separated, and only buy one month's supply at a time as large quantities often deteriorate.

Feeding Methods

Horse owners must decide not only *what* to feed, but how and when. The horse's diet must include enough bulk—if not grass, then hay. If stabled and exercised, he needs short feeds three or four times a day, at regular times. Boredom in the stable encourages bad habits. A good feeder takes about 20 minutes to eat an average feed, then one and a half hours to digest it. Allow for this if he is to be ridden after a feed, or make it smaller. Hay is bulky, so feed it after work, and at night. If it is fed loose on the floor, choose a dry, clean place, but haynets are best for controlling amounts.

Never give a large feed to a hungry horse.

If dust makes your horse cough, or thick-winded, soak or damp his hay.

Always remove stale, wet or uneaten feeds from the manger.

Horses kept in a covered yard should have continuous access to hay and fresh water, and be fed at regular times to avoid fighting. A timid horse may be bullied at feed times; he may have to be fed separately.

(*Above*) **Hay racks** should be easy to reach. Falling seeds irritate eyes and nostrils.
(*Below*) **Haynets** are convenient, and adjustable: tie at eye-level using a quick-release knot.

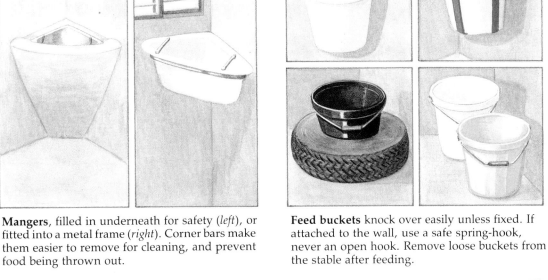

Mangers, filled in underneath for safety (*left*), or fitted into a metal frame (*right*). Corner bars make them easier to remove for cleaning, and prevent food being thrown out.

Feed buckets knock over easily unless fixed. If attached to the wall, use a safe spring-hook, never an open hook. Remove loose buckets from the stable after feeding.

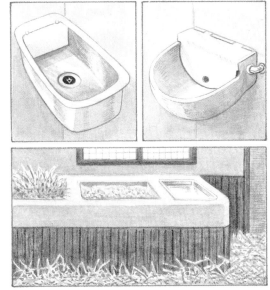

(*Top left*) Stream with sound access; (*top right*) stagnant pond, should be fenced off; (*below left*) self-filling trough; (*below right*) sharp-edged, dirty, hand filled bath.

Automatic drinking bowls save labour but may block up or freeze. Also, how much is being drunk? Mangers combined with a water-bowl need to be emptied and cleaned regularly.

Making up Feeds

A skilful feeder will give each horse exactly what he needs to keep him in prime condition—no more and no less.

Until you can judge quantities accurately, weigh each ingredient.

An unbalanced diet or an over-large feed of concentrates could prove disastrous.

If a scoop or bowl holds 2 lb (900 g) of oats, the same scoop holds around 2 lb (900 g) coarse mix (according to the brand), 2¾ lb (1.2 kg) cubes, 1 lb (450 g) bran, 3 lb (1.3 kg) uncooked whole-grain barley.

Feeds should have a crumbly texture not dusty, nor be a wet, paste-like mess. Always mix roughage with cereals: chaff, sugar-beet pulp or low-energy nuts make the feed easier to digest and more beneficial. If any part is musty or stale, a horse may reject the whole feed. Fresh green food, or carrots or apples, and salt, are necessary for stabled horses.

Food and exercise must balance, but at least 25% of any horse's diet must be roughage.

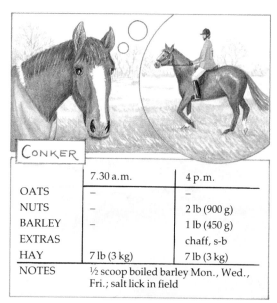

CONKER

	7.30 a.m.	4 p.m.
OATS	–	–
NUTS	–	2 lb (900 g)
BARLEY	–	1 lb (450 g)
EXTRAS	–	chaff, s-b
HAY	7 lb (3 kg)	7 lb (3 kg)
NOTES	½ scoop boiled barley Mon., Wed., Fri.; salt lick in field	

Sample feed for 13 hh pony kept out in a field in **winter** but working weekends and school holidays.

JAKE

	7.30 a.m.	12.30 p.m.	4 p.m.	8 p.m.
OATS	2 lb (900 g)	2 lb (900 g)	4 lb (1.8 kg)	3 lb (1.3 kg)
NUTS	–	1 lb (450 g)	1 lb (450 g)	1 lb 450 g)
BARLEY	–	–	1 lb (450 g)	–
EXTRAS	–	–	chaff, s-b	–
HAY		10 lb (4.5 kg)	–	10-12 lb (4.5-5.5 kg)
NOTES	p.m. vitamins, carrots, ½ scoop boiled barley alternate days or if very cold			

Sample feed for 16 hh horse working hard in **winter** (stabled).

AMBER

	7.30 a.m.	4 p.m.
OATS	–	½ lb (225 g)
NUTS	1 lb (450 g)	1 lb (450 g)
BARLEY	½ lb (225 g)	1 lb (450 g)
EXTRAS	½ lb (225 g) bran	–
HAY	–	–
NOTES	Give hay only if in a bare paddock.	

Sample feed for 13-14 hh pony in **summer**, regularly working off grass.

Cooked Food

Most horses and ponies enjoy *boiled barley*, fed warm as a supplement to a regular feed, or with bran. It adds variety and is excellent for putting on condition, especially in winter.

A *bran mash* is a mild laxative. It is fed *warm*—not scalding hot!—and is suitable for a fit horse the night before he has a rest day. A plain bran mash is not very appetising: add a handful of molasses, and/or sliced apples or carrots, some boiled barley, linseed, a few oats/crushed barley, and a tablespoon of salt.

A mash is useful for administering medicine or worm doses.

Linseed is very rich in oils. It should be fed sparingly, as a jelly, mixed with the normal feed. It is beneficial in winter and ideal for show horses who need fattening up and a glossy coat. Linseed tea, the excess liquid in which it was cooked, is also highly nutritious, and useful for making a bran mash.

Cover the **barley** (up to 1 lb (450 g) per horse) with boiling water (or steam in a sieve). Bring to the boil. Simmer for 4–6 hours. The grains will split and swell.

Put one handful of **linseed** per horse, in a saucepan, and soak it in water overnight. Add more water — about 2 pints (or 1.2 litre) — boil and simmer. Allow it to cool and set into a jelly.

Fill two-thirds of a bucket with **bran**. Soak it thoroughly with hot water. Cover, and leave to cool. Mix in 1–4 oz (25–100 g) salt, and other ingredients, and feed while still warm.

Food and Fitness

A horse is said to be in GOOD CONDITION if flesh covers his bones and his coat shines. He is in SHOW CONDITION when he carries more fat and looks rounded and glossy. A muscled-up horse with no spare flesh or fat, is in FIT CONDITION; but a thin horse with wasted muscles is in POOR CONDITION.

Condition can alter very quickly, and much depends on the balance between food and work. Native-type ponies, for instance, take plenty of exercise searching for their food. In a good summer they may look fat and well, but in winter they are much thinner, even if fed extra hay. The same ponies, when moved on to good quality pasture, will do well in winter but become grossly fat in summer and their grazing must be controlled to avoid laminitis. Less hardy ponies, and most horses, will thrive on good summer grass, but will need more concentrates in winter, as well as hay.

When horses are working, the amount and type of food must be adjusted, to provide the necessary energy. An idle, 'soft' horse may look healthy, but his muscles are slack and he carries excess fat. To work him too hard, or fast, too soon is likely to overburden his legs and unprepared muscles, or to strain his lungs and heart. Also, the fat is used and disappears before muscle has time to build up, leaving a thin, weak horse. It will take several weeks of slow, progressive exercise to get him fit.

Horses working from grass, or stabled at night only, can need the same amount of concentrates as fully stabled, fit horses—or even more in severe weather.

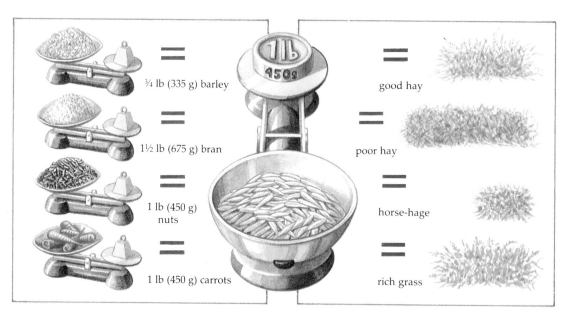

¾ lb (335 g) barley

1½ lb (675 g) bran

1 lb (450 g) nuts

1 lb (450 g) carrots

good hay

poor hay

horse-hage

rich grass

Concentrates

Roughage

Signs of Good Health

A healthy horse looks alert, with eyes open wide and bright, and ears pricking to and fro. His coat shines and his skin feels supple and loose. Sweating for no obvious external reason, and rapid or noisy breathing, are bad signs. His pulse rate should be about 40 beats per minute, and he should breathe at a rate of about 12 inhalations per minute when at rest. His droppings, passed approximately eight times per day, should split on hitting the ground. They will vary in colour between golden brown and dark green, according to his diet, but should not be coated in slime or smell offensive. A horse at grass has loose droppings, but not sloppy like cow-pats. Urine should be passed several times a day and should be pale yellow in colour.

A keen appetite and good digestion are vital to a horse's health. Poor condition is usually caused by bad feeding, fatigue, or ill-health. His teeth should also be examined and his droppings analysed for worms.

A horse in 'soft' condition, with a grass belly and slack, weak muscles. He is not fit and will become distressed if worked. His coat looks dull and wormy.

Extreme loss of weight is usually due to lack of suitable food, overwork, faulty digestion, teeth problems, severe worms, or pain in the mouth or elsewhere.

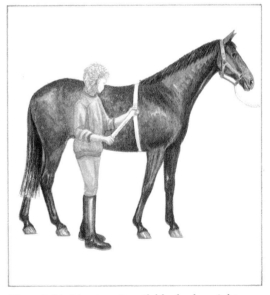

If a weighbridge is not available, bodyweight can be estimated with a marked weigh-tape, as above, e.g. a horse measuring 69 ins (175 cm) should weigh 1000 lb (454 kg).

17

Suitable Types of Diet

When the grazing is good, horses living out during spring and summer need no other food. As the amount and quality of grazing lessens, they will need hay, preferably fed in haynets or racks. Loose hay on the ground is often wasted: it blows away, or becomes trampled and soiled. Hard food becomes necessary for most horses and ponies in wet, cold weather when they use up energy to keep warm. It should be fed in strong bowls or portable mangers—not buckets, which will tip over.

How much concentrates to feed will depend on the weather, and the individual. Hardy ponies need less than non-native types of the same size, especially when there is plenty of good grazing. Old horses and very young ones need more energy-giving food than a mature animal in good condition. A highly-strung horse tends to lose weight, but oats will not help; he needs high-protein nuts, maize, sugar-beet pulp and cooked barley and linseed, or, alternatively, a suitable coarse mix. If his appetite is poor, take the trouble to find out what he likes.

Other sources of warmth must also be considered: i.e. whether the horse is rugged up, clipped and rugged, and whether he has good shelter from wind and rain.

Stabled horses which do not work can be maintained on hay only. Good quality hay provides more than enough energy and warmth to keep them looking and feeling well.

A horse in light work needs about 30% concentrate, with 70% hay; in moderate work he needs 40%–50% concentrates with 60%–50% hay; and in hard or fast work, 70%–75% concentrates with 30%–25% hay. Again, these figures will vary slightly, according to the individual and his size and weight.

Sample feed charts for a working 15 hh horse are shown here.

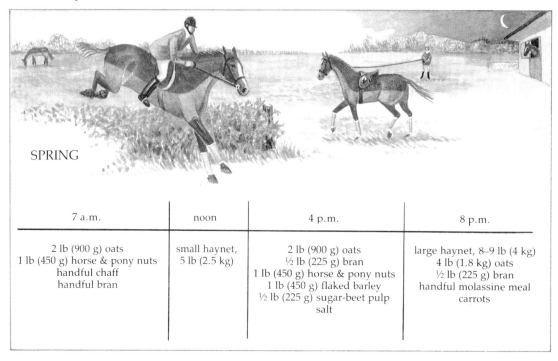

SPRING

7 a.m.	noon	4 p.m.	8 p.m.
2 lb (900 g) oats 1 lb (450 g) horse & pony nuts handful chaff handful bran	small haynet, 5 lb (2.5 kg)	2 lb (900 g) oats ½ lb (225 g) bran 1 lb (450 g) horse & pony nuts 1 lb (450 g) flaked barley ½ lb (225 g) sugar-beet pulp salt	large haynet, 8–9 lb (4 kg) 4 lb (1.8 kg) oats ½ lb (225 g) bran handful molassine meal carrots

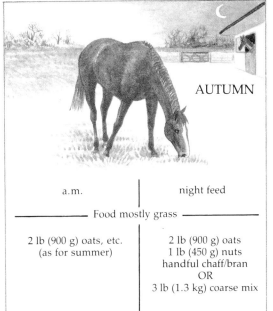

SUMMER

a.m.	p.m.
— Food mostly grass —	
2 lb (900 g) oats OR 2 lb (900 g) flaked barley OR 2 lb (900 g) horse & pony nuts OR 1 lb (450 g) grain + nuts sugar-beet pulp	2 lb (900 g) oats (as a.m.) 2 lb (900 g) horse & pony nuts ½ lb (225 g) bran/chaff + salt

AUTUMN

a.m.	night feed
— Food mostly grass —	
2 lb (900 g) oats, etc. (as for summer)	2 lb (900 g) oats 1 lb (450 g) nuts handful chaff/bran OR 3 lb (1.3 kg) coarse mix

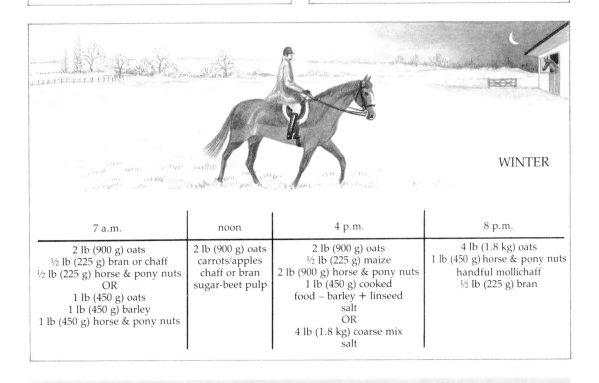

WINTER

7 a.m.	noon	4 p.m.	8 p.m.
2 lb (900 g) oats ½ lb (225 g) bran or chaff ½ lb (225 g) horse & pony nuts OR 1 lb (450 g) oats 1 lb (450 g) barley 1 lb (450 g) horse & pony nuts	2 lb (900 g) oats carrots/apples chaff or bran sugar-beet pulp	2 lb (900 g) oats ½ lb (225 g) maize 2 lb (900 g) horse & pony nuts 1 lb (450 g) cooked food – barley + linseed salt OR 4 lb (1.8 kg) coarse mix salt	4 lb (1.8 kg) oats 1 lb (450 g) horse & pony nuts handful mollichaff ½ lb (225 g) bran

Feeding a Sick Horse

When a horse who normally enjoys his food loses his appetite, he is probably not well. He should be stabled, to 'nurse' him and monitor his eating and drinking.

A sick or injured horse will need a light, nourishing and attractive diet, with no concentrates until he has recovered. Good, fresh grass is the ideal tonic, but avoid lawn mowings as they overheat and are indigestible. Prepare small, tasty feeds at about four-hour intervals.

A bran mash is useful, being mildly laxative. Linseed jelly helps to make it more appetising and nutritious, as would succulents, molasses, or sugar-beet pulp. Chaff will ensure that he chews properly.

If the horse is coughing, or has respiratory problems, damp or soak his hay and dampen his feed slightly. Never leave uneaten food in the manger, and always supply clean, fresh water and mineral salt.

A sick or injured horse who has no exercise should be fed 'soft' food: hay, or horse-hage, fresh cut grass, and bran mashes made as palatable as possible.

It is kinder to keep ponies on very limited rations than to let them get too fat on rich grass, risking laminitis. Give plenty of water.

A 'poor doer' never looks really well, despite every effort to make his food more appetising. To solve this problem, the reason 'why' must be discovered.

Feeding and Breeding

Breeding stock should be in good, rather lean condition, but not fat. Brood mares of every type can thrive on good grazing until it loses its value in early autumn, when extra hay should be fed. Through the winter they will need a high protein diet, including cereals, maize and linseed or a compound of these, to build tissue and muscle for the foal's development.

While the vital protein, starches, fats and roughage are found in grass, or hay, and cereals, important minerals—such as calcium for bone growth—are supplied by sunshine, herbage and soil. Very rich fertilised grass makes youngstock grow too fast, with soft, spongy bone; poor grass will stunt their growth.

During the cold winter months they will need energy-giving foods to maintain healthy growth. A good brand of youngstock cubes will include all the nutrients, but will not suit every type of horse or pony. If in doubt, seek expert advice.

A Thoroughbred stallion, like a competition horse, needs up to 16 lb (7 kg) of hard food plus best hay, for maximum fertility, and regular exercise to keep him fit.

Fibrous roughage, or bulk, should form at least half of a brood mare's diet, to help absorb the protein. The amount of bulk can be varied according to her figure.

When grass is at its best, a mare and foal need little else, but when the grazing is poor, a high protein diet and good hay should keep the milk flowing.

Food and Health

Bulk foods keep a horse's digestive system in running order, and concentrated foods build muscle and provide energy. The right balance is vital.

Avoid working a horse hard on too much bulk: it strains his lungs and heart, as well as his legs. Too much grain in relation to work, on any one day, can cause indigestion (a serious problem in horses) and chemical changes which can lead to colic, azoturia, lymphangitis, and laminitis. In most cases, a laxative should ease the symptoms, but seek veterinary help.

The benefits of good feeding will be lost unless the horse's teeth are in good condition to chew it and digest it properly, and unless he is wormed regularly every six to eight weeks. Worms eat his food and get into the bloodstream, causing loss of weight and anaemia. Damage to the bowel, and in bad cases, his liver, lungs and blood vessels, can be serious and long-term.

A **'wormy'** horse loses condition, has a dry, staring coat and sometimes a pot-belly. Worm doses are given as paste (*above*), or in powder form added to a feed.

Colic is acute indigestion, often due to over-feeding, eating unsuitable food, a sudden change of diet, water *after* feeding, or too much cold water when hot.

A horse's **teeth** grow throughout his life. They must be checked at least once every year by a vet, farrier, or specialist horse dentist, to rasp away sharp edges.

Lymphangitis often affects just one hind leg, which swells badly, starting at the hock and spreading along the entire leg. It is very painful and may cause fever.

Azoturia, or **set-fast**, usually attacks the hindquarters of a fit horse which, after a 'rest' day in his stable on full working feed, seizes up when exercised.

Filled legs, swollen with fluid, are a sign of poor blood circulation or congestion, often caused by too much food in relation to the work being done.

Laminitis is a painful fever in all the feet, mostly affecting ponies allowed too much grass, or stabled horses fed too much heating food without enough exercise.

Storage

A horse is very particular about what he eats and drinks. He is unlikely to feed on mouldy forage, poisonous plants or grass treated with weed-killer. However, access to these could be dangerous, as an extremely hungry or greedy horse is less fussy.

Rat poisons (or rat droppings) may also cause serious illness and should be avoided if possible. Employ a good stable cat!

Feed charts for every horse should be marked up clearly, to prevent mistakes being made.

The different types of feed should be identified perhaps by writing on the bins. These should always be emptied of old food, and cleaned before re-filling.

Whole grain keeps well in dry, cool conditions, but rolled or crushed grain should be consumed within two to four weeks.

Keep food utensils clean and the floor swept.

An electric power point will be useful for boiling water.

Keep feed in vermin-proof bins, with heavy or strongly secured lids. Rats and mice *must* be controlled, as they will eat and contaminate food and spread disease.

Good food is wasted unless stored in a dry, clean place. Damp food deteriorates quickly, and mouldy food is poisonous. Dirty floors attract vermin and bacteria.

Hay and straw should be stacked on pallets, or slats, to allow air to circulate underneath and to preserve the lowest bales from damp. Wet hay soon becomes mouldy.